USBORNE FIRST
Level Three

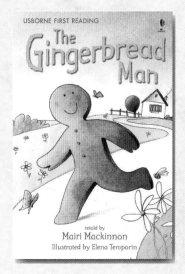

USBORNE FIRST READING

The Gingerbread Man

retold by
Mairi Mackinnon
Illustrated by Elena Temporin

USBORNE FIRST READING

Bugs

Sarah Courtauld
Illustrated by Daniela Scarpa

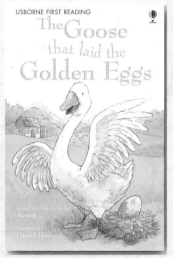

USBORNE FIRST READING

The Goose that laid the Golden Eggs

based on the fable by
Aesop

Illustrated by
Daniel Howarth

USBORNE FIRST READING

The ENORMOUS TURNIP

based on the story by Alexei Tolstoy
Illustrated by Georgien Overwater

frogs

Sarah Courtauld

Illustrated by Jacqueline East

Reading Consultant: Alison Kelly
Roehampton University

Splosh!

A frog dives into a pond.

It swims fast, kicking out
its strong back legs.

Whoosh!

On land, frogs use their legs to hop around. They jump from spot to spot.

All frogs need water to stay alive. They don't drink it.

It creeps in through their
slimy skin.

7

Each week, they change
their skin.

They wriggle and jiggle
out of the old one.

Underneath, there's a new
one – all slimy and wet.

Frogs live all over the world. There are frogs in deserts, living under the sand.

They only come out when
it rains.

There are
frogs in
rainforests,

climbing
trees.

They cling on
with their sticky feet...

12

then

g l i d e down

to the ground.

All frogs eat bugs. Some
leap up to catch them.

Some use their sticky
tongues.

A fly buzzes past...

The frog flicks out its
tongue and snaps it up.

Frogs come in lots of sizes.
The smallest frog is as tiny
as a raindrop.

The largest frog is as big
as a cat.

Some animals eat frogs.
But frogs have tricks to
get away.

This snake is attacking a
tomato frog.

The frog makes a sticky
white goo. It tastes horrible.

The snake
slithers away, hissing.

This frog sees a bird coming.
It blows up

bigger

and bigger

and bigger.

The bird is too scared to
eat it... and flies away.

Dogs only like eating
live frogs.

So, this frog pretends
to be dead.

The frog waits.

The dog
runs off.

The frog hops away.

Once a year, many frogs
go on a long journey.

They hop back to the pond
where they were born.

At last, they arrive.

Croak!

Croak!

Croak!

The male frogs sing to
the females.

Some frogs sing very loudly.

Kerrouk!

Krok!

Kraaaarrrk!

You can hear them for
miles around.

28

Green tree frogs sound like loud bells.

Some frogs make a
tinkling sound.

Tinkle

Tinkle

Tinkle

Yap!

Others sound like dogs.

30

There are even frogs that sound like people snoring.

After singing, the male
and female frogs get
into pairs.

Then the female lays eggs
in the water.

At first, the eggs are tiny dots.

Soon they hatch into wriggling black blobs called tadpoles.

The tadpoles are very,
very hungry.

They eat all the plants
they can find. Then they
start to change.

First they grow back legs.

Then they grow
front legs.

Their long tails shrink.

Now they are little frogs, called froglets.

They hop and leap and splash in the pond.

In a few weeks, they
leave the pond.

One day they will
come back...

and have froglets of
their own.

Froggy fact

Some frogs go to sleep
in winter.

They freeze,
and their
hearts stop
beating.

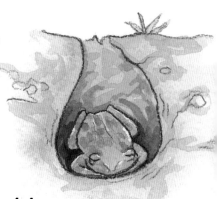

In spring, they leap back to life and hop outside.

Froggy words

Here are some of the words in the book you might not know.

 tadpole - a baby frog

 froglet - a young frog that is not fully grown

 glide - to float along in the air

Index

Frog websites

You can find out more about frogs by
going to the Usborne Quicklinks Website at
www.usborne-quicklinks.com and typing in the key
words "first reading frogs". Then click on the link
for the website you want to visit.

The recommended websites are regularly reviewed and updated but,
please note, Usborne Publishing is not responsible for the content of
any website other than its own. We recommend that young children are
supervised while on the internet.

Edited by Susanna Davidson

Designed by Zoe Waring

Series editor: Lesley Sims

Consultant: Chris Mattison

First published in 2007 by Usborne Publishing Ltd., Usborne House,
83-85 Saffron Hill, London EC1N 8RT, England. www.usborne.com
Copyright © 2007 Usborne Publishing Ltd.

USBORNE FIRST READING
Level Four

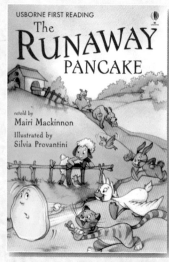